Dear God, What About Me?

A 30-Day Devotional
for Single Women

ALENA GOVAN

A *Singles Living 4 Him* Publication

Dear God, What About Me? A 30-Day Devotional for Single Women
Copyright © 2018 by Alena Govan

All rights reserved. This book or any portion thereof may not be reproduced or used in any manner whatsoever without the express written permission of the author except for the use of brief quotations in a book review.

For more information:
- On the web, go to singlesliving4him.blogspot.com
- Or via email, contact jesussaveseva8@gmail.com

Scripture quotations marked (NIV) are taken from the Holy Bible, New International Version®, NIV®. Copyright © 1973, 1978, 1984, 2011 by Biblica, Inc.™ Used by permission of Zondervan. All rights reserved worldwide. www.zondervan.com The "NIV" and "New International Version" are trademarks registered in the United States Patent and Trademark Office by Biblica, Inc.™

Scriptures marked KJV are taken from the KING JAMES VERSION (KJV): KING JAMES VERSION, public domain.

Cover and interior graphics by Sarah Smith
Edited and formatted by Rachel L. Hall

Printed in the United States of America
First Edition, 2018
ISBN-13: 978-0692155271
ISBN-10: 0692155279

*To my Heavenly Father,
for walking with me and encouraging me
through this journey of my life
and future journeys to come.*

*To my loving parents, John and Merle Govan,
for teaching and guiding me in the Christian faith.
Your love and support have allowed me to become
the woman I am today.*

Contents

Introduction	ix
Day 1: COMPARISON	1
Day 2: WORRYING ABOUT WHAT OTHERS THINK	5
Day 3: TEMPTATION	8
Day 4: LONELINESS	12
Day 5: FROM FEAR TO THANKSGIVING	16
Day 6: IDOLS IN OUR LIVES	20
Day 7: DISAPPOINTMENT	23
Day 8: ANGRY WITH GOD	27
Day 9: WHY?	30
Day 10: FORGIVING OURSELVES	34
Day 11: FORGIVING OTHERS	38

Contents

Day 12: BLAME — 42

Day 13: PURPOSE — 46

Day 14: HEALTH — 50

Day 15: PURITY — 53

Day 16: PRAYER — 56

Day 17: FASTING — 59

Day 18: SPIRITUAL WARFARE — 62

Day 19: HAVE FUN — 66

Day 20: DOING KIND DEEDS — 70

Day 21: FINANCIALLY FIT — 74

Day 22: MOTIVE — 77

Day 23: LOVE — 81

Contents

Day 24: PATIENCE	84
Day 25: JOY	87
Day 26: FAITH	90
Day 27: SELF-CONTROL	93
Day 28: PRAISE AND WORSHIP	96
Day 29: PEACE OF MIND	99
Day 30: ART OF CONTENTMENT	102
Conclusion	107

Introduction

Hi Reader,

Jump in the passenger seat of this Honda Civic—or any car of your choice—as you travel on this road trip to contentment. (I love Honda Civics, by the way.) As you travel, allow God to be the driver. Let Him speak to you on this journey. Then you will gain even more insight than what I provide in this book.

Studying this devotional will enlighten you: you are not the only one to face issues that are in fact common to single women. Sometimes as a single person in a world which seems dominated by couples, you may feel as if others are not going through the same problems you are. But often they are.

For each day, I've provided a prayer for you to use. Each prayer is meant simply as a guide, so you can add to the prayer as you desire. You'll find a Course of Action for each day as well. Use it to reflect and see if there is something in your life that you may want to work on. As you devote yourself to prayer and reflection through these devotionals, you may want to consider fasting anytime during the thirty days.

Of course, some of the topics covered are not what you as a single Christian woman may face. You may already know your purpose, and maybe you never experience being angry with God. Yet I would encourage you to read and pray through the book in its entirety—even topics that you don't deal with. Maybe you can be a help to someone else who is struggling with these topics. For the topics that you are dealing with, write in the spaces provided in this devotional or in a journal how you plan to implement each course of action.

Who Am I?

What qualifies me to write to the unsatisfied single woman? I am qualified because I know her. I am qualified because I was the embodiment of this woman. I know all the hurts, pains, joys, and rejections of this woman, so I can write to her.

Being single for as long as I have been was never in my plans. I thought I would be married by twenty-five years old. Twenty-six came, then twenty-seven… Talk about disappointment! But God had other plans. As I write this book, I'm still single with no prospect of getting married.

I pray that what I've learned along the way will be a blessing to you. This journey is not an easy one, but it's the road that God placed me on to help single, unsatisfied women find their way to contentment. And it's the road He's placed you on (at least for now!) and you will discover peace in that through devotion to Him.

My prayer is that this book will give you hope and encouragement. While I can't promise that you will reach complete contentment in thirty days, I pray that you will learn and grow as you travel on this road.

~Alena Govan

Dear God, What About Me?

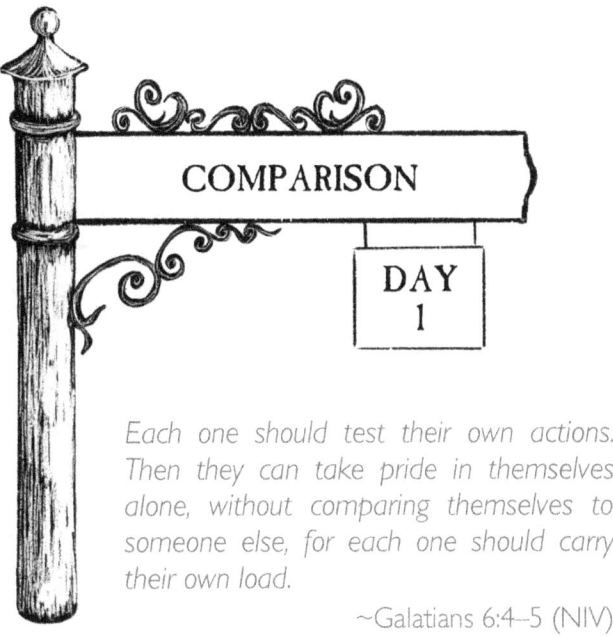

COMPARISON

DAY 1

Each one should test their own actions. Then they can take pride in themselves alone, without comparing themselves to someone else, for each one should carry their own load.

~Galatians 6:4–5 (NIV)

Birds chirp outside my window as sunrays flood my room, reminding me that morning has come. I quickly grab my smartphone and check my social media pages. As I scroll down the screen, I see announcements of engagements, weddings, baby arrivals—the list goes on. I'm left feeling, "That's great! But what about me?"

My fresh start to the day is slightly tainted. Insecurities begin to arise. I worry a bit. "When will I be able to post such happy announcements?" I wonder. I find myself playing the comparison game. Big mistake.

Social media is not reality. Most of the time people reveal only the good experiences that occur in their lives. The vacations, weddings, parties, promotions, new homes, new cars, etc., are merely the highlights of most peoples' lives. Those picture-perfectly filtered moments lead us to believe that others have their lives so much more together than we do. When we don't have what they have, we begin to think that something is missing from our own lives.

Marilyn Monroe, from the outside looking in, appeared to have had it all—beauty, money, and fame—but in a 1960 interview with *Marie Claire* magazine, she made a statement: "Do I feel happy in life? I'm not generally happy. If I'm generally anything, I guess I'm generally miserable."

Comparing your life with others' is a waste of time and energy for two reasons. First, what looks good for someone else may not be good for you, and second, you don't know their whole story. Consider Marilyn Monroe: many wanted her success, fame, and appearance, but I'm sure they wouldn't want to have her problems.

Many live believing the saying, "The grass is greener on the other side of the fence." The solution to this mindset is to water your own grass to make it greener. In other words, if you want to see changes in your own life, take appropriate steps to fulfill your desires. There's nothing wrong with thinking or even saying, "Oh I would like to have a family like that," or "I want to have abs like that."

Day 1: Comparison

But when we start thinking that we want a person's *life*, problems arise.

The sad truth is that comparison can lead to jealousy and envy. We have all felt this in one way or another. It looks as if everyone's life moves along like flowing water while we are stuck in a deep hole trying fruitlessly to climb out.

Where is God in all of this? He is right there, walking beside you, waiting for you to give Him your undivided attention. He wants us to stop comparing our lives to others' and look at Him.

Take time to pray this:

Prayer

Lord, thank You for providing all of my desires thus far and in the future. When the spirit of jealousy or envy arises, remind me of Your love and promises. Thank You for blessing those around me with their hearts' desires. Constantly remind me that life isn't a race to see who can get married first or who can have their first child first. My journey will look different than others' journeys, but my journey is one that is just as beautiful. In Jesus' name. Amen.

Course of Action

For the next 30 days, instead of allowing negative thoughts to whisper lies such as "You are less than…," "This will never happen for you as it happened for them," or "You are unworthy," each day write down three things that God has done for you.

Start today!

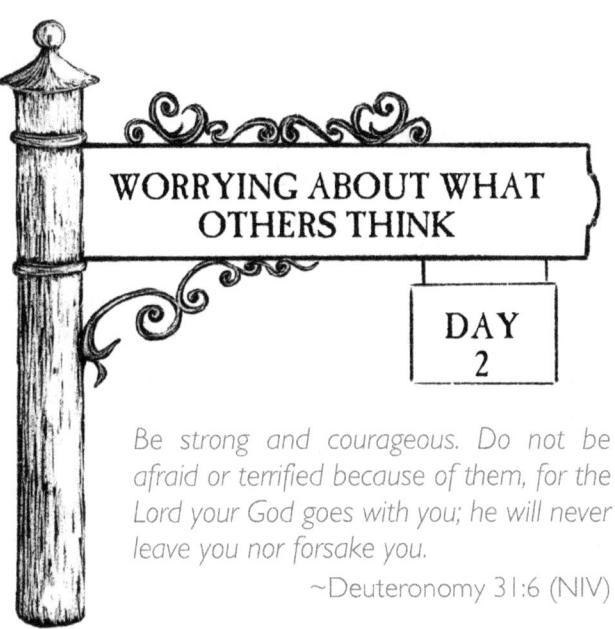

WORRYING ABOUT WHAT OTHERS THINK

DAY 2

Be strong and courageous. Do not be afraid or terrified because of them, for the Lord your God goes with you; he will never leave you nor forsake you.

~Deuteronomy 31:6 (NIV)

The white, cold blanket of snow outside starkly contrasts the warmth coming from the fireplace inside a quaint, cozy cottage. Its occupants enjoy the warm smell of gingerbread cookies in the oven accompanied by the sweet and creamy taste of hot chocolate. Pine trees decorated with a mixture of homemade and store-bought ornaments stand tall in the center of the room.

All signs point to a beautiful Christmas holiday. However, they can be a painful reminder of thoughts such as "I'm single again—another year of not inviting a husband or boyfriend to a family Christmas dinner." Conversations at the dinner table are sure to turn to you: "So when are you getting married? When are you going to have some babies?"

Holidays, whether Christmas, Thanksgiving, or Valentine's Day, are hard for a lot of singles. During these times, you may need to gently remind yourself that it's not your time to have a partner, and it's okay. You don't have to prove anything to anyone, and your worth as a person is not dependent on whether or not you are part of a couple.

If being asked when you are going to start a family bothers you, realize that most who ask are probably coming from a good place. They don't mean to hurt you and they are genuinely concerned about you. People are often not aware of your sensitivity concerning this topic.

God wants us to trust Him completely and to stop worrying about the opinions of others.

Let's pray.

Prayer

Lord, I pray that constant worry of what others think will dissipate. I acknowledge that Your will for my life is good and perfect. I pray for the people who constantly feel the need to remind me to get married and have children. Lord, help me to not take their remarks personally, but allow it be an opportunity to be a witness for Your name. In Jesus' name. Amen.

Day 2: Worrying About What Others Think

Course of Action

The next time someone asks you when you will get married and start a family, tell them with confidence that you trust that it's all in God's timing. If the person is not a Christian, you may have an opportunity to witness to them. Show them through your reactions and responses that in the Christian walk we are to trust God in every area of our lives.

Try it now! Write out a response to a question you hear frequently which bothers you, such as: "Do you have a boyfriend yet?" In your answer, state your trust in God.

TEMPTATION

DAY 3

There hath no temptation taken you but such as is common to man: but God is faithful, who will not suffer you to be tempted above that ye are able; but will with the temptation also make a way to escape, that ye may be able to bear it.

~1 Corinthians 10:13 (KJV)

After Jesus fasted for forty days and forty nights in the wilderness (Matt. 4:1–11), the devil appeared and tempted Jesus three times. The first time the devil said to Him, "If you are the Son of God, tell these stones to become bread." The second time he said, "If you are the Son of God, throw yourself down." The third and final time he said, "All this I will give you, if you will bow down and worship me."

Jesus responded to each temptation with the Word of God.

It's important to note that Jesus was tempted during one of his weakest moments here on earth, right after He fasted. This is like us today. The

Day 3: Temptation

enemy may tempt you when you are weak and when you are most vulnerable.

How can we overcome temptations? The first step is to recognize our temptations. Modern temptations people face include sexual temptations, overeating, procrastination, and abusing drugs/alcohol. What may be a temptation for one person may not be a temptation for the next.

For instance, one person will feel tempted to spend countless hours on social media whereas another person may spend just a few moments catching up with close family and friends' posts.

Those who find themselves lost in scrolling through social media may have procrastination as a root cause. It is easy to be tempted to procrastinate: we put off completing more important tasks for a later time or date, convinced we "need" to know what's happening on media feeds, scared we'll miss something important. But by procrastinating, whether through social media use or other temptations we face, we can cause ourselves stress.

Once we recognize our temptations, we need to stay away from putting ourselves in situations where we know we will be tempted.

Another crucial step to overcoming temptations is to speak the Word of God like Jesus did. If fornication is a weakness, use Scripture such as 1 Corinthians 6:19. If gossiping about other people is a temptation, use Ephesians 4:29.

Of course, we can and should simply ask God to help us whenever we are faced with temptation.

Through the process, He may direct us to fast about these temptations as well.

Temptations are inevitable and we will encounter them. Think about it: if Jesus was tempted, you know temptations will come your way. It's important to note, though, that although Jesus was tempted, He never sinned.

Let's pray.

Prayer

Father God, I ask that You give me the strength to overcome every temptation that arises in my life. When the enemy plants these temptations, I know that Your Spirit will guide me on how to deal with them. In Your precious name, Jesus. Amen.

Course of Action

What are some of your biggest temptations in life? Asking the Holy Spirit to help you, determine a strategy to deal with those temptations. For example, if you deal with fornication, you can avoid being alone with a guy in his place of residence at night.

Start by writing down one of your temptations, and begin to find a practical strategy to deal with it now.

Day 3: Temptation

Temptation:

Strategy from the Holy Spirit:

LONELINESS

DAY 4

...[Teach] them to obey everything I have commanded you. And surely I am with you always, to the very end of the age.

~Matthew 28:20 (NIV)

A tall metal wall had risen up around my heart. Behind it, I became isolated and ultimately lonely. People in my support group would ask me, "How are you doing?" And I would say, "Fine," knowing deep down I wasn't. I had put up the wall, mistakenly believing that I could take care of my issues myself.

Loneliness is a battle I have faced during my single season. I know loneliness first hand, and I believed its lies for so long: "If only I had a boyfriend, I wouldn't be lonely," and "Once I get married, my loneliness will vanish!"

What we as single women sometimes fail to realize is that loneliness is not an emotion that only we battle. Loneliness is not limited to marital status,

Day 4: Loneliness

gender, race, ethnicity, or creed. You can be in a room full of people and still feel lonely. A person can be married and still feel lonely.

How can we overcome loneliness? First, we must evaluate our relationship with Christ. A stable relationship with Christ is the primary foundation for eradicating loneliness. He promises, "And I will ask the Father, and he will give you another advocate to help you and be with you forever… I will not leave you as orphans; I will come to you" (John 14:16,18).

If our relationship with Christ is well, our next step is to reach out to others we know for support. We can meet new people, and committing to being an active part of a community—especially among believers—is vitally important.

It is not God's desire that we isolate ourselves from others. Scriptures, including Ephesians 4:11–13 and Acts 2:42, encourage us to be an active part of the body of Christ. One purpose in being part of the body is so that we can build up and encourage one another. In Hebrews 10:24–25, it states: "And let us consider how we may spur one another on toward love and good deeds, not giving up meeting together, as some are in the habit of doing, but encouraging one another—and all the more as you see the Day approaching" (NIV).

Why do we isolate ourselves? We isolate ourselves at times because we feel like others may not understand what we are going through. We may also isolate ourselves because of the fear of rejection. But loneliness stems from not connecting with others, and the wall we've begun to place around our hearts gets bigger the more we let loneliness take control.

If we are brave enough to share our hearts with those in our support system, we may discover that the walls we've built will start coming down and loneliness will begin to disappear. While I am not an advocate of sharing all of your problems with everyone, there will be times when God gives you a platform to share your struggles. Your support system is the people that you trust and you know who love and support you. This support group may offer up prayer, advice, and love when you need it most.

God does not want us to feel lonely. When we start to feel lonely, we need to go to God and ask Him to remove that emotion. God is always there with us. Even if we feel family members, friends, co-workers, etc., have forsaken us, He is constantly there.

Take time to pray this:

Prayer

Lord, I ask that You remove the spirit of loneliness and in its place engulf me with Your Holy Spirit. Father, I ask that You surround me with people whom I can foster great relationships with. In place of the wall I've built, encircle me with the right people in my life so that I can be a blessing to them.

Day 4: Loneliness

Course of Action

When we take our eyes off ourselves and look at what God wants us to do in His Kingdom, loneliness can disappear. The prayer for today mentions surrounding yourself with the right people whom you can bless. List some ways in your community, church, job, etc., that you already are a blessing, and then list some ways that you can be a blessing to others.

So, think about it: who do you bless now? Who can you bless? What does that do to your sense of loneliness?

How I am a blessing:

_____
_____
_____
_____
_____

How I can be a blessing:

_____
_____
_____
_____
_____

FROM FEAR TO THANKSGIVING

DAY 5

Trust in the Lord with all your heart and lean not on your own understanding.

~Proverbs 3:5 (NIV)

As a single woman, when I first entered my late twenties, I began to ask, "What if I never get married?" I would think, "I don't want to end up all alone!" Thoughts like these would plague me at times. Truthfully, I was afraid of what was going to happen—or not happen—in my future. Sometimes, such thoughts still try to tempt me today, but using the Word of God to remind me that He holds my future in His hands helps me a great deal. It's not always easy to do, but I trust God with my life.

We sometimes create goals such as:

Day 5: From Fear to Thanksgiving

- Will be married in 5 years;
- Will start my business in 2 years;
- Will have my first child at age 26;
- Will have the all-American dream home with a white picket fence and 2 ½ children by 30.

When these check-list items are not manifested in the timeframe we anticipate, we become discouraged. We often wonder if we are doing something wrong.

Wait, you say, I'm 25, 30, 40, 50, or even 70, and I'm not married yet. How could I not be discouraged? What's going to happen to me? But you are a child of God, and God has your life perfectly mapped out. Our self-made plans do not always align with what God has for us and they may not even be in our best interests. When misalignment shows up, we have to shift our perspective and trust that the plan of God is perfect—more perfect than we could ever imagine.

When fear cripples us, we cannot appreciate what is happening in our lives right now. God taught me to enjoy the intricate details of today and to allow Him to be the writer of my future. For instance, He has taught me to enjoy the people currently in my life. The time we have today cannot ever be relived again. A conscious and intentional appreciation of the present will begin to replace fear of the future.

How can I be thankful when I feel unsatisfied? One way is to stop concentrating on what I don't have and look around me at what I do have. We have so much to be thankful for, and yet sometimes we get in a rut of moping around with thoughts like "Why am I still single? Why am I not blessed like everyone else?"

So, unsatisfied woman, don't concentrate on what you don't have. Embrace God's blessings. You might get tempted to complain, and that is natural. But practicing being grateful for the present season that you are in will allow you to learn satisfaction in what God has given you. After all, if you can't be thankful in the now, will you be really thankful in the future, no matter what God gives you?

Let's pray.

Prayer

Lord, I don't know what is going to happen in my future, but I know that You hold my future in Your hands and are crafting it perfectly according to Your will. When I'm in fear that life may not go according to what I have planned, I will remember Your unfailing love and Your perfect plans for me. Lord, remove fear from my heart and replace it with the faith to know that all things are working for my good.

Day 5: From Fear to Thanksgiving

Course of Action

What are some of your fears about the future? List them.

My fears:

_____

_____

_____

_____

_____

Ask God to help you deal with these areas of your life. Meditate on Scriptures dealing with fear. When thoughts of fear enter in your mind, speak the Word of God against fear. Look up Psalm 55:22, Psalm 34:4, Mark 5:36 and others that address your fear(s). Now, write down the word God has for you.

God's promise to me:

_____

_____

_____

_____

_____

IDOLS IN OUR LIVES

DAY 6

Thou shalt have no other gods before me.
~Exodus 20:3 (KJV)

What do you think about when you hear the word *idol*? Perhaps images of statues of false gods come to your mind. Merriam-Webster defines *idol* as an "object of extreme devotion and a much loved or admired person or thing." Idols are more than just statues of false gods: they can be everyday things and even people that we put above the one and only true God. Modern idolatry can include spending endless hours on social media following the latest beauty and fashion trends, a focus on acquiring wealth, obsessing over celebrities, and the list goes on.

There's nothing inherently wrong with social media, acquiring wealth, or even looking up to a

Day 6: Idols in Our Life

celebrity. Any of these can become a problem, though, when they get in the way of our relationship with God. Anything which distracts you from your time with or focus on God becomes an idol.

Get this! The guy you are in a relationship with or the guy you just secretly like can become an idol to you. Even the idea of getting married can be made into an idol if we constantly obsess over it.

Scriptures reveal that God is a jealous God. We need to be mindful that we do not consume our time or money with things that are not of God. When Jesus tells the Samaritan woman at the well that "whosoever drinketh of the water that I shall give him shall never thirst," He isn't referring to natural water but to a spiritual truth that provides complete satisfaction (John 4:14 KJV).

The truth about idols is they will never give you complete satisfaction because that only can come from God.

Take time to pray this:

Prayer

Father God, I ask that You reveal to me any idols in my life. I ask Your Holy Spirit to help me not put these objects, ideas, fascinations, etc., above You because I know that You are the true and living God. In Jesus' name, I pray. Amen.

Course of Action

What are the idols in your life? To help answer this question, consider things in your life that cause you to brush aside spending time with God. Make a list of these items.

Idols in my life:

_____
_____
_____
_____
_____

Confess these items to God and repent. Repeat today's prayer, and after you say this prayer, take specific steps to remove the idol. For instance, if your idol is spending a lot of time on social media, give yourself a break from it or limit the amount of time you use it.

How I will break my idols:

_____
_____
_____
_____
_____

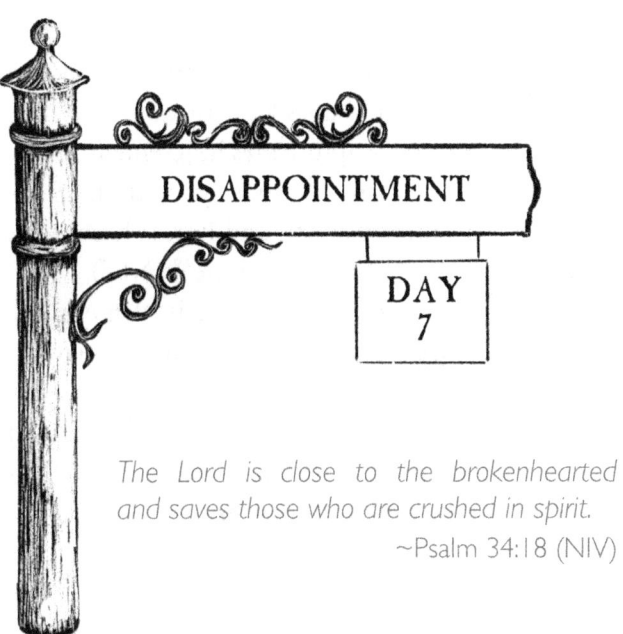

The Lord is close to the brokenhearted and saves those who are crushed in spirit.
~Psalm 34:18 (NIV)

The email read, "We have completed our interview process and filled the position with an individual who has significant experience."

What? How could that be? I knew in my heart that I killed the interview. *Disappointed* is putting it mildly to describe how I felt. It had been a year since I graduated from college, and I still had no job. I was heartbroken. This was yet another of what now felt like countless job opportunities I had applied for. Once again, I had been rejected.

We have all felt disappointment. Maybe you were in a relationship that you thought would last for a long time, only to realize it wasn't meant to be. Maybe you received bad news from the doctor concerning your health. Disappointment comes in many forms, but what does God say about it?

I love what the Scripture says in Jeremiah 29:11. "'For I know the plans I have for you,' declares the Lord, 'plans to prosper you and not to harm you, plans to give you hope and a future'" (NIV).

You probably wonder how hope is even possible when you experience disappointment. We have to keep in mind that feelings are not truth. God's Word is truth! When you feel like God is against you, reciting Scriptures like Jeremiah 29:11 reminds you of God's good plans for you.

Disappointment and heartbreak are the unexpected visitors that catch us unaware. The truth about heartbreak is that there is always a hidden gem accompanied with it. Sometimes, you may have to look very closely with a magnifying glass, but it's there. How can it be? You wonder, "How can the thing that caused my heart to break be a gem? Unfathomable." Yet a broken heart can birth wisdom. It can birth growth. It can birth patience. And one day if you look even deeper, it will birth an unexplainable joy. If you allow it, disappointment and heartbreak can shed a layer of negative pride from your life, and in its stead, humility can come. It can shed a layer of indifference and replace it with compassion.

The bottom line? Learn from your disappointment and let your broken heart be the catalyst for healing. Then move on.

Day 7: Disappointment

Take time to pray this:

Prayer

Father God, I come humbly in Your presence to ask that You surgically remove the disappointment lodged in my heart. Although I may be left with a small visible scar, the scar will remind me that You healed my heart from disappointment. As I go out into the world, may my scar be a blessing to others as I share the miracles You work out through my life. In Your precious name, Jesus. Amen.

Course of Action

What are some disappointments that have occurred in your life? Write them down.

Major disappointments:

_____
_____
_____
_____
_____
_____

Ask God to heal you of those disappointments by proclaiming His truth. Recite 1 John 3:1, Romans 8:28, and John 3:16 aloud:

Dear God, What About Me?

For God so loved the world that he gave his one and only Son, that whoever believes in him shall not perish but have eternal life. (John 3:16 NIV)

And we know that in all things God works for the good of those who love him, who have been called according to his purpose. (Rom. 8:28 NIV)

See what great love the Father has lavished on us, that we should be called children of God! And that is what we are! The reason the world does not know us is that it did not know him. (1 John 3:1 NIV)

Let these Scriptures be your meditation when you deal with disappointment.

ANGRY WITH GOD

DAY 8

He throws me into the mud,
and I am reduced to dust and ashes.
I cry out to you, God,
but you do not answer;
I stand up, but you merely look at me.

~Job 30:19–20 (NIV)

As I sat kneeling before God on the cold floor that somehow mirrored my heart, I had no words to pray. The truth was that I was angry with God.

As tears slowly ran down my face, I whispered, "Jesus, I don't have the words to pray. My heart is completely shattered." My body shook as I began to weep, not knowing what to say to God at this point. "How could you have allowed this, God?"

In trials, you can find yourself being angry with God. I've experienced that anger. I've been angry because I've been hurt and didn't understand why certain events took place. Yet even though I was angry and hurt, I couldn't stop talking to Him. I wanted to know how could God allow this to happen. It has helped me to realize that even when I don't know the why, I need to trust in God no matter the circumstance.

During moments of anger, the enemy attacks your mind on whether you should turn your back on God. We live in an imperfect world where bad things happen to good people. If bad things happen to good people, we may find ourselves asking, "Is it even worth it to live for Christ?" "Where is my reward for living for God when tragedy just crashed into my present?"

We know that one day going to heaven is a reward, but in the moment, all we feel is anger. I've wrestled with these thoughts only to come to the conclusion that if God allowed a loss, a tragedy, a disappointment to occur in a child of God's life, it will come back and work out for good in the end.

Let's pray.

Prayer

Father God, help me to understand that Your ways are not my ways and Your thoughts are not my thoughts. Help me, Father, to trust You more than ever. Sometimes, the pain can be so much that I may not have the words to pray, but Lord, I know that if I just call on the sweet name of Jesus, that is enough. When I call on Your name, You will come and I know You will comfort me. I may not understand why this has happened, but my anchor is in You. In Your precious name, Jesus. Amen

Day 8: Angry With God

Course of Action

What do you do when you are angry with God? Admit to God that you are angry with Him for said reason. Many people are afraid to be honest with Him. God knows that you are angry with Him, so admit to Him how you feel. Keep a conversation with Him, no matter what. Tell Him, "Lord, I'm angry with You." If that's all you can say at that moment, then do it. If you have no words, read passages from the Bible, especially Psalms which give thanks to God. Repeat those words. Keep yourself encouraged by going to church, reading His Word and possibly even talking with a pastor or Christian counselor, or a trusted friend.

Take time now to examine your heart. Are you angry with God? Tell Him. If not, pray that He would give you the courage to always be honest before Him.

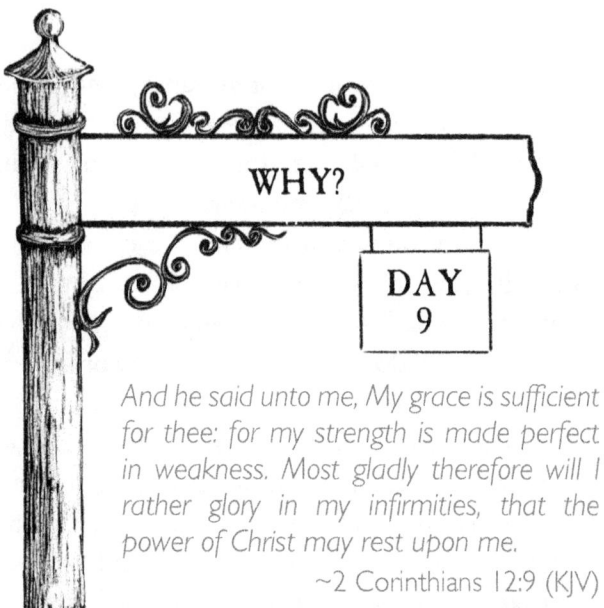

WHY?

DAY 9

And he said unto me, My grace is sufficient for thee: for my strength is made perfect in weakness. Most gladly therefore will I rather glory in my infirmities, that the power of Christ may rest upon me.

~2 Corinthians 12:9 (KJV)

For years, I've pondered the *why* in circumstances that were beyond my control. Why didn't I get married younger? Why did this person in my life have to die? Some of the answers I have yet to find out.

Whys make me think of Job. In the beginning of the Book of Job, Job is described as "perfect and upright, and one that feared God, and eschewed evil" (Job 1:1 KJV). *Eschewed* means "to depart from," so we know Job kept away from evil. The Scripture goes on to tell us that this perfect, upright, God-fearing, evil-eschewing man had a large family and was wealthy (vv. 2–3). It seems everything was perfect for Job.

Day 9: Why?

Satan approached the Lord and they began discussing Job. The Lord, like a father proud of his child for doing well in life and for being morally right, praised Job, saying that he was perfect (v. 8). Satan responded, "Duh—of course he will serve You because You have given him so much, but take all that he has and he will curse you."

The Lord granted Satan permission to touch Job's possessions, but He told Satan that he couldn't kill Job. One by one, Job began to suffer extreme loss, including his children and his possessions. To top it off, he began to suffer physically.

Yet Job never cursed God. His wife, overcome with grief due to all they'd lost, even told him, "Curse God and die" (2:9).

Job responded, "You are talking like a foolish woman. Shall we accept good from God, and not trouble?" (2:10 NIV). Job, we are told, didn't sin in what he said about all that was going on. He was firmly grounded in his faith.

His strong faith, however, didn't stop him from questioning God. He wanted to know the *why*. What could he have done to deserve such calamity? Indeed, no one around him could fathom the idea that such terrible things could happen to someone who was living right before God. Time after time, his friends accused him of hidden sin. Their prideful questioning led Job's finite mind to be undoubtedly confused and troubled.

In the end, God doesn't answer Job's *why* questions. Instead, He asks Job a series of questions, including this one: "Where were you when I laid the earth's foundation? Tell me, if you understand" (38:4 NIV). In other words, God informs Job that he doesn't have the full knowledge and wisdom of this world because Job's understanding is limited.

The truth of the matter is you may never understand the *why* behind loss and disappointment. Guess what? It's okay. If you're anything like me, I used to feel like I always needed to know the *why* to every disappointment, but then God told me that I didn't have to.

Today, I'm giving you the freedom of not knowing the *why* either. I'm giving you the freedom to stop racking your brain for the answers. God wants us to have an open line of communication with Him, and it's natural to question Him. But if He doesn't answer, trust Him. It's easier said than done, but a weight will be lifted from you if you do.

Let's pray.

Prayer

Holy Spirit, help me to settle my mind concerning the *whys* in my life. Lord, if it's Your will for me to know the answers, please reveal them to me. If not, I ask that You constantly remind me that I am loved through it all. In Your precious name, Jesus. Amen.

Day 9: Why?

Course of Action

What are some *why* questions you have? How do you plan to settle them? Write down your responses and trust God with His responses.

My *whys?*

Ways I can trust God in response:

FORGIVING OURSELVES

DAY 10

If we confess our sins, he is faithful and just to forgive us our sins, and to cleanse us from all unrighteousness.

~1 John 1:9 (KJV)

Mark, a high school student, had aspirations of becoming a teacher. He was preparing to make that dream a reality until his girlfriend informed him that she was pregnant.

"Here's the deal, Mark. Either we are going to get married or I'm going to have an abortion," she told him.

Mark stood there, stunned after hearing the news that would change the course of his life forever. Deep down, he knew abortion was wrong. But when he was faced with the situation himself, he knew he didn't want to get married yet. He

Day 10: Forgiving Ourselves

agreed to the abortion. They went through with it, and he was ridden with guilt about their choice.

After sleepless nights, he decided to go to church. When he went, he learned about God's grace, mercy, and forgiveness. He knew he couldn't change what happened, but he began to accept God's forgiveness.

The Scriptures address the importance of forgiving others, but many of us remain plagued with not forgiving ourselves. After repenting for a sin, we overanalyze something that we did in the past and feel guilt over what God has already forgiven us for. When we hold on to past sins, we can't move on with our lives in a positive way. In other words, we become stuck. Why do we torture ourselves with past sins?

The answer to that question comes down to another question: do we really believe that God forgives our sins? If we do, we must live in that truth. So, if the enemy tries to torment you with past sin which you've already repented from, counteract those thoughts with the Word of God. First John 1:9 says, "If we confess our sins, he is faithful and just to forgive us our sins, and to cleanse us from all unrighteousness" (KJV). If God can forgive us our sins, we must forgive ourselves. Say it out loud: "God has forgiven me."

I love this passage of Scripture: "For all have sinned, and come short of the glory of God" (Rom. 3:23). In other words, none of us has lived without sinning against God. It is in man's nature to sin, so don't be too hard on yourself. But if you have sinned, ask God to forgive you, and then walk away from the sin.

Let's pray.

Prayer

Holy Spirit, I know I can't change the past of what I have done, but Your Word says, "If we confess our sins, he is faithful and just to forgive us our sins, and to cleanse us from all unrighteousness." This passage of Scripture stands true. Even if the enemy tells me I am not forgiven, Your Word says that I am.

Course of Action

Do you have trouble forgiving yourself? If so, speak the Word of God over your life. Meditate on the following Scriptures, and then search out more on forgiveness.

- Jeremiah 31:34 (NIV)

> "No longer will they teach their neighbor,
> or say to one another, 'Know the Lord,'
> because they will all know me,
> from the least of them to the greatest,"
> declares the Lord.
> "For I will forgive their wickedness
> and will remember their sins no more."

Day 10: Forgiving Ourselves

- Psalm 103:12 (NIV)

    *As far as the east is from the west,
    so far has he removed
    our transgressions from us.*

FORGIVING OTHERS

DAY 11

Bear with each other and forgive one another if any of you has a grievance against someone. Forgive as the Lord forgave you.

~Colossians 3:13 (NIV)

Thwack. A sharp stone hit his left arm. He winced and reflexively grabbed at the stinging spot with his right hand. *Thwack.* Another hit his leg. *Thwack. Thwack.* He braced himself as the stones came faster. Stephen called out to the Lord, "Lord, do not hold this sin against them."

Mind-blowing, right? How is it possible to ask for someone else's forgiveness as they are killing you? That can only be done through the Holy Spirit. The story of Stephen in Acts 7 is a remarkable example of forgiveness in the Bible.

Stephen was falsely accused of blasphemy against Moses and God by the Synagogue of the Libertines, Cyrenians, Alexandrians, and some of

Day 11: Forgiving Others

Cilicia and Asia. Once the gossip of his alleged blasphemy circulated, the council questioned him. Stephen didn't defend himself, but instead gave an account of Abraham and Moses, letting the council know that the Israelites resisted the Holy Spirit and persecuted God's prophets, just as they were doing with Stephen. The council was offended, and they began to stone Stephen.

In situations where people hurt us, most of us react in defense: "Punish them for what they are doing to me! Matter of fact, I want to be there when they are punished." Come on, you know you have felt like that. While it is a challenge and takes great integrity and strength to fight for a cause or even be willing to die for someone, to ask for forgiveness for someone who is in the act of killing you is unimaginable.

So how do you actually forgive someone when they hurt you? When I've been hurt by another, God has told me to pray for the person. My immediate response is, "But I don't want to." And His response is, "It will be good for you to pray for the person."

When you pray for someone that hurts you, it releases the anger you have built up towards the person. The Word of God says in Matthew 5:44, "But I say unto you, Love your enemies, bless them that curse you, do good to them that hate you, and pray for them which despitefully use you, and persecute you." When I pray for those who have hurt me, it releases what I had in my heart against them and God enables me to love them in a godly manner.

Take time to pray this:

Prayer

Lord, I ask that You bless _____ (*insert name of the person who hurt you*). I ask that You erase the hurt that they have caused me. Lord, if You are able to forgive me for what I have done, I believe that You will equip me to forgive those who hurt me. Allow my heart not to be hardened by their actions but to instead remain soft with Your overflowing love. In Jesus' name. Amen.

Course of Action

Are there people in your life whom you have trouble forgiving? If so, pray for these individuals. This may take time, so don't give up if forgiving someone may take longer than you expect. Continue calling out their name in prayer and watch what God does.

Name the person or write out the past hurts:

_____
_____
_____
_____
_____

Day 11: Forgiving Others

Now, write your prayer for those individuals:

I will praise thee;
for I am fearfully and wonderfully made:
marvellous are thy works;
and that my soul knoweth right well.

~Psalm 139:14 (KJV)

"If I was this size, I would be married by now."

"If I was prettier, I would be married by now."

"If I wasn't so picky, I would be married by now."

Excessive *if* statements plague many single women. All the *ifs* leave them feeling more frustrated than ever about their current marital status. I have had *if* statements run through my mind at times, and like so many other single women, I blamed myself for being single.

I blamed myself for not being in the place where God wanted me to be. I thought fasting might hopefully speed up the process of being single.

Day 12: Blame

Maybe if I fast, I thought, then God will reveal to me what I need to work on to become the wife for my future husband. As I grew in my faith, God taught me that fasts are not about manipulating Him, but about growing closer to Him.

I attended single women's conferences in hopes of learning how to be the wife for my future husband. I've read books, watched YouTube videos, and read countless articles. I listened to others' testimonies to see what they did to get their husband. You name it, and I probably tried it. I was in pursuit of marriage as if there was some type of formula to achieve that goal.

I wanted to know not just the secret to getting a husband, I wanted to know the secret to getting a godly husband. We all can get married, but to marry the man that you've prayed for for years was the challenge.

I finally realized that it wasn't healthy to blame myself, that it wasn't good to try to manipulate God, and that obsessively pursuing finding a husband was getting me nowhere. One day God had me stop the blame game. He spoke to my heart about purpose. Instead of vigorously pursuing marriage, I allowed Him to begin to teach me the importance of purpose. I began to stop blaming myself for being single because I learned that where I am is where God wants me to be for His purpose. Blaming yourself for being single wreaks havoc not only on how you feel about yourself but it can ultimately damage your relationship with God.

Let me ask you this. Do you think that all the women who are married in godly relationships are where they need to be spiritually? Just because a person is married doesn't mean he or she has the whole Christian lifestyle mastered. Even when you do get married, you will still be working on areas in your life. The best thing to do is be the best woman of God you can be by living out God's Word in your life—not to get a man, but to please the Father.

Let us pray.

Prayer

Holy Spirit, I ask that You come to my rescue every time I blame myself for being single. If there are areas in my life that I need to change, I ask that Your Spirit guide and instruct me. Instead of blaming myself for being single, God, let me be the best woman of God that You have ordained me to be. I am not living this godly life to secure a husband but to satisfy You. Father, keep reminding me that I am wonderfully and fearfully made by You. In Jesus' name. Amen.

Course of Action

If you are anything like me and have blamed yourself for being single, let it go! Yes, there are areas in our lives that we need to work on whether we are single or married, but ask God to help you

Day 12: Blame

in those areas. Recite Psalm 139:14 when the "*If Statements*" enter your mind.

I release my *ifs:*

_____
_____
_____
_____
_____
_____
_____
_____
_____
_____
_____
_____
_____
_____

I speak aloud the following:

> *I praise you because*
> *I am fearfully and wonderfully made;*
> *your works are wonderful,*
> *I know that full well.*

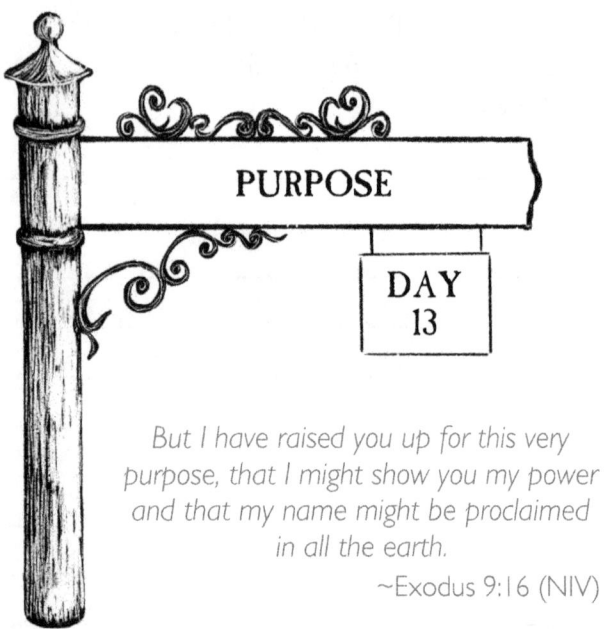

PURPOSE

DAY 13

But I have raised you up for this very purpose, that I might show you my power and that my name might be proclaimed in all the earth.
~Exodus 9:16 (NIV)

Solomon pours out his heart when he declares, "Meaningless! Meaningless!… Utterly Meaningless! Everything is meaningless!" in the first chapter and second verse of the book of Ecclesiastes (NIV). To a first-time reader of the book, the statement paints the author as a pessimist, a person who views life as half-empty, or worse. While Solomon's views cause the reader to question his negative outlook, Solomon brings to light the truth that some people's lives mirror what amounts to leading a meaningless life. They adopt the attitude that nothing really matters, so they might as well live it up while they have the chance. They

Day 13: Purpose

adopt promiscuous lifestyles, not thinking about the consequences of their actions.

Solomon "denied nothing his eyes desired," yet he still felt unsatisfied. This wisest man who ever lived later concludes that life with God *is* fulfilling. The key to filling the emptiness is God.

We are tempted to believe that once we attain certain dreams, goals, and possessions we will be satisfied. Once we have children our lives will not be empty; if we have that great career, life will be complete. Even if these desires are indeed good, if we are empty inside before attaining them, we will still be empty after. This is why it's so important to seek God for your purpose.

Walking in purpose counteracts the idea of life being meaningless. Knowing our purpose answers the questions, "Why are we here?" and "What is the point of it all?" We become alive in our purpose, awakening as a blossoming flower emerges from a small seed. The seed of faith must first be planted. That seed is believing that you are a child of God created for a purpose.

Don't be afraid to walk in purpose. The path to fulfilling your purpose may be difficult and intimidating. Purpose may lead you to travel out of your comfort zone, but ultimately, your purpose is one that you will enjoy. It is something that others can't choose for you, but it is one that through the guidance of the Holy Spirit will eventually be revealed to you.

Prayer

Father God, allow me to become aware of the purpose that is quietly hidden in me. I ask that You connect me with the right people who will help me flourish in my purpose. When life feels meaningless, cause me to remember that You have a tailor-made purpose in my life.

Course of Action

Write down the things you are passionate about. Maybe you have a passion to help underprivileged youth or help the homeless. What is that thing that burns in your heart that gives you so much joy? Once you find it, you have been introduced to your purpose.

My passions:

Day 13: Purpose

What God is revealing to me about my path to purpose:

Keep traveling, friend!

*Beloved, I wish above all things
that thou mayest prosper and be in health,
even as thy soul prospereth.*
~3 John 1:2 (KJV)

According to the Centers for Disease Control, the leading causes of death in the United States today are heart disease and cancer. In our Christian walk, we stress the importance of living for God, but taking care of the body that God has given us is important as well. The Word of God says that our bodies are the temples of the Holy Ghost. Do we treat our bodies with that in mind? Prevention is one of the key things to living a healthy lifestyle.

Here are some steps we can incorporate to make sure that we are healthy:

1. Eat healthy
2. Exercise

Day 14: Health

3. Go to the doctor for yearly checkups
4. Drink more water
5. Get enough rest

It's important to make small improvements first when it comes to taking care of our body. For some that may mean slowly backing away from fast food and sugary foods. Practice being active, but do something that you enjoy because if you enjoy the activity, you will be more likely to continue it.

Exercise should be fun and not a bore. In my search for great workouts, I discovered indoor spin classes. I was hesitant because many people cautioned me that the classes were intense, but I decided to try it anyway. Guess what? I found out that I absolutely love taking spin class. Don't be afraid of trying something new. If an activity is intriguing, even if it looks intimidating, at least give it a try.

When we are healthy, we have the strength to minister to others. Our body will have the strength it needs to carry out the tasks that God has for us. If we are unhealthy, carrying out those tasks may be very difficult to do. Let's say this prayer together.

Prayer

Dear Heavenly Father, I ask that You give me the wisdom to take care of this temple. My body, this earthen vessel, is one that I desire to use for Your glory, but in order to do that, I need to be healthy physically, mentally, and emotionally. In Your precious name, Jesus. Amen.

Course of Action

What are you going to do to become healthier or to continue a healthy lifestyle? Hire a personal trainer, join a gym, come up with a meal plan, etc. Write down your health goals and find ways to implement them.

My Health Goals:

_____
_____
_____
_____
_____

Steps to Achieve those Goals:

_____
_____
_____
_____
_____
_____
_____

PURITY

DAY 15

Finally, brethren, whatsoever things are true, whatsoever things are honest, whatsoever things are just, whatsoever things are pure, whatsoever things are lovely, whatsoever things are of good report; if there be any virtue, and if there be any praise, think on these things.

~Philippians 4:8 (KJV)

Men and women wearing barely anything pose on magazine covers, leaving little room for the imagination. Some popular music addresses women as if they are objects to conquer rather than people to treasure.

When we think about purity, most people associate the word with sex. But purity is more than just sex. It's a way of life. Purity is not just for singles. Purity is not just for women. God wants even married couples to live a pure life before Him. In Philippians 4:8, Paul advised those in the church thousands of years ago: "whatsoever things are pure…think on these things."

How can we focus our thoughts on pure things in a world saturated with images of living a life so contrary to purity? Purity begins in the heart of a believer. We can monitor where we go, what music we listen to, what shows and movies we watch, what books we read, etc. Once we decide that we will not participate in certain activities, through the help of the Holy Spirit our actions will follow.

A close friend told me that if she invited Jesus for a ride in her car and it would be embarrassing for her to listen to the music in front of Him, then she wouldn't listen to it at all. That is a perfect way to consciously choose to live in purity. Remember: purity is not about legalism—it's about relationship. If you feel God convicting you that something leads you away from purity, then listen to what God is telling you.

It's not always easy to live differently from everyone else. One thing I try to remember is that I'm not here to please man. I'm here to please God. With that mindset, the choice to do well is easier.

Take time to pray this:

Prayer

Lord, I ask that You continuously clean me with hyssop that I will be whiter than snow as Your Word states in Psalms 51:7. Lord, I ask that You make my mind, actions, and words pure so that I will be pleasing to You. Teach me continuously how to live pure. Convict me of things that are

Day 15: Purity

currently in my life that are contrary to walking in purity. In Jesus' name, I pray. Amen.

Course of Action

If you deal with lust or other impure thoughts or actions, ask yourself what you are feeding your spirit that pertains to lust. Are you watching media, listening to music, or reading books that feed the impurity? If so, ask God to help you stop entertaining those things and then make the required steps to stop.

This desire for heart purity is a creation of the Holy Spirit at work in the heart.

Duncan Campbell
(Scottish Revivalist, b. 1898–d. 1972)

PRAYER

DAY 16

*Devote yourselves to prayer,
being watchful and thankful.*

~Colossians 4:2 (NIV)

BEEP. BEEP. BEEP.

My alarm clock went off at 5:30 AM. I reached over to hit the snooze button and quickly dozed back to sleep.

BEEP. BEEP. BEEP.

"Ugh," I uttered as I threw the warm covers over my head. "Just 5 more minutes," I reasoned. I hit the snooze button again. This time, I wasn't able to fall back to sleep. Then I became angry with the alarm clock.

BEEP. BEEP. BEEP.

As I headed out the door, I realized that I forgot to pray, so to help ease my mind I quickly said a simple prayer. Am I the only person who finds

Day 16: Prayer

themselves in situations like that? The ten extra minutes I had for sleep (unsuccessful, at that) could have been used for praying. I must admit I find myself in those situations more often than I'd like.

We have relationships with our family, friends, church members, etc., and the key to any type of relationship is communication. If we stop communicating with a loved one or the communication becomes less and less frequent, the relationship suffers. The importance of communication in a relationship with Christ—also known as prayer—is just as vital and even more so than in our relationships with others. We cannot grow in our spiritual walk if we don't commune with the Heavenly Father. It's not about how long we pray: it's the sincerity of our heart that God looks for. We *can* make time with God, because we make time for what we want to make time for.

As single women, we can certainly make time to spend with Christ. Once we are married and have children, we may find ourselves struggling to even find five minutes to ourselves. So, we should take advantage of this time, now. Doing so will help us establish time with Christ as a priority for the rest of our lives. If not now, when?

During these special prayer times with Him, we learn more and more about His love and grace. He imparts wisdom and love into our spirits so that we can be equipped to deal with life in general.

One of the keys to answered prayers is faith. In Mark 11:24, Jesus says, "Therefore I tell you, whatever you ask for in prayer, believe that you have received it, and it will be yours." When you pray, pray words from your heart. Share with Him all the most intimate details of your life that you may be afraid to share with other people. His shoulder is the best one to lean on.

Let's pray.

Prayer

Jesus, I ask that You continue to speak to me throughout Your Word and in my heart. Give me the wisdom to use my time wisely so that I will be able to spend more time with You. In Jesus' name. Amen.

Course of Action

If your prayer life is not where you want it to be, think of ways you can improve your prayer life. Get up earlier in the morning or use your spare time in the evenings instead of watching social media, TV, etc. Begin to use some of that time to pray to God.

When I can pray:

_____
_____
_____
_____
_____
_____

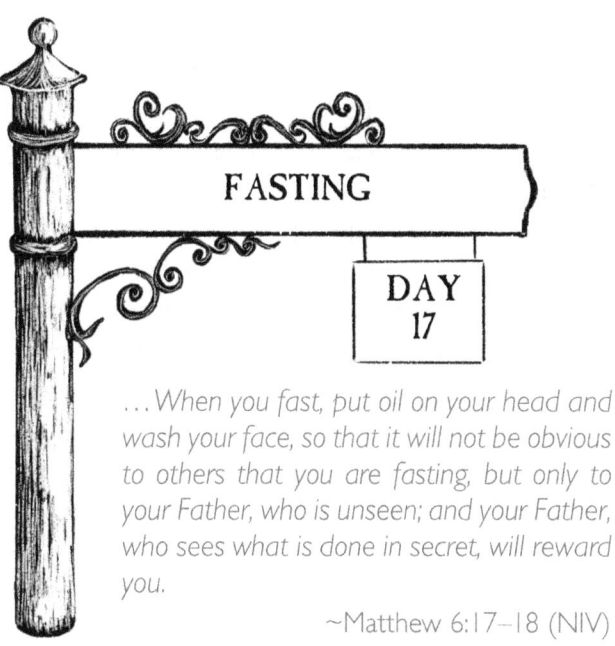

...When you fast, put oil on your head and wash your face, so that it will not be obvious to others that you are fasting, but only to your Father, who is unseen; and your Father, who sees what is done in secret, will reward you.

~Matthew 6:17–18 (NIV)

"I just can't do this Christian life anymore," exclaimed Sharon to her best friend Paula. "God still hasn't given me a husband yet after I have patiently waited for Him to do so. I haven't slept around since giving my life to Christ seven years ago, and yet God hasn't rewarded me for my good behavior." Sharon and Paula are both 20-something Christian, single women.

"I know it's hard, Sharon, but we have to keep trusting God that He will give us the desires of our hearts," Paula said. Paula felt in her spirit that both the women should go on a fast. "How about this? Let's go on a fast."

"Fast?" exclaimed Sharon. Her spiritual life lately had been in a serious drought. Sharon knew that she should fast because truth be told she hadn't fasted in a long time. But she felt resistant. "Why should I fast? Am I fasting for a husband now?"

"No: we are fasting to build our spiritual muscles to learn to wait on God. We are fasting to become closer to Him, so we won't become distracted by what we don't have," Paula answered.

After considerable thought, both women agreed to fast.

Fasting is practiced in religions worldwide, such as Islam, Buddhism, and of course Christianity. Nonreligious and spiritual people alike may fast for medical reasons as a prevention or treatment for illness. Others fast to protest a cause. In the Word of God, we find examples where individuals from the Old and New Testament fasted. But, should we fast today, and what is the purpose, you may ask?

Yes, we should fast. In denying our flesh food for a defined period of time, we focus on growing spiritually and come closer to God. Jesus fasted for forty days and forty nights. As believers, if our purpose is to be like Jesus, we should practice what He did while He was here on earth, and that includes fasting.

Fasting can bring forth breakthroughs that we probably wouldn't experience if we didn't fast. In the story of the demon-possessed boy found in Mark 9, the disciples had trouble driving out the spirit possessing him. When Jesus intervened, He

Day 17: Fasting

rid the boy of the evil spirit. Afterwards, the disciples asked Jesus why they were not able to drive the spirit out. The Lord replied to them, "This kind can come forth by nothing, but by prayer and fasting" (v. 29 KJV).

When you do fast, you must pray for your fasting to be effective. This is the time where you commune with God, speaking to Him and listening as He reveals more of Himself to you.

Let's pray.

Prayer

Dear Father, as I fast, I ask that You strengthen me to go through with the fast. The spirit is willing but the flesh is weak. As I fast, draw me closer to You that I may flourish into the woman that you want me to be. I ask that You reveal more of Yourself to me during this time. In Jesus' name. Amen.

Course of Action

If you want to get to know God on a deeper level, try incorporating fasting into your life. You can start with fasting half of the day, and as you grow in Christ, you may be led to longer fasts. The spiritual benefits from fasting are simply amazing.

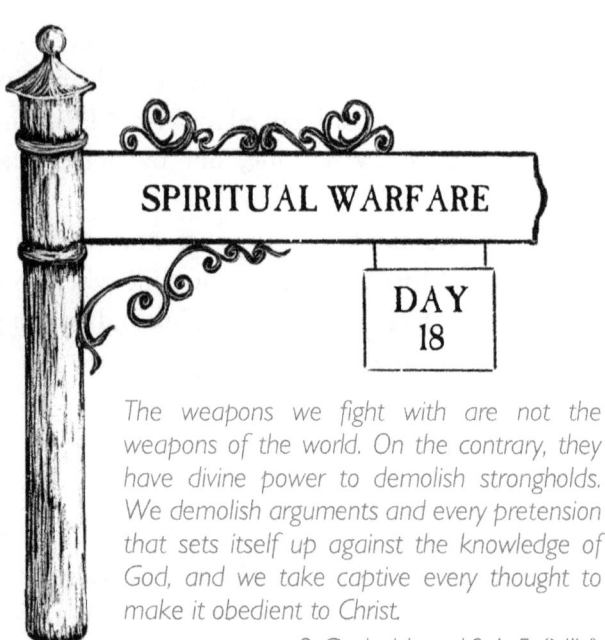

SPIRITUAL WARFARE

DAY 18

The weapons we fight with are not the weapons of the world. On the contrary, they have divine power to demolish strongholds. We demolish arguments and every pretension that sets itself up against the knowledge of God, and we take captive every thought to make it obedient to Christ.

~2 Corinthians 10:4–5 (NIV)

As soldiers go out prepared for battle with the right weapons and garments, believers must go out into the world with spiritual weapons and garments. In Ephesians 6:10-17, Paul urges the church to put on the full armor of God. He lists each piece of armor: the belt of truth, breastplate of righteousness, feet fitted with the readiness that comes from the gospel of peace, shield of faith, helmet of salvation, and sword of the Spirit. Each piece is a spiritual weapon that we must use to fight when circumstances or even people come up against us.

Day 18: Spiritual Warfare

As singles, the devil sometimes tempts us with thoughts of fear, worry, lust, and everything that is against the Word of God. We must fight those thoughts with these spiritual weapons.

- **Belt of Truth**—As the enemy whispers lies to us, the belt of truth is there to thwart those lies by replacing it with God's truth which is found in His Word.
- **Breastplate of Righteousness**—When Satan comes in and says that we are not worthy and we are unrighteous, remind him of 2 Corinthians 5:21—"For he hath made him to be sin for us, who knew no sin; that we might be made the righteousness of God in him."
- **Feet fitted with the readiness that comes from the gospel of peace**— If we keep our feet fitted with the readiness that comes from the gospel of peace by studying God's Word and being in His presence, when the opportunity comes for us to witness, we will be ready.
- **Shield of Faith**—Always keep the shield of faith ready for when the enemy may tempt us to believe that God is not real or that He won't come through with His promises.
- **Helmet of Salvation**—Our helmet of salvation needs to always be on: "For by grace are ye saved through faith; and that not of yourselves: it is the gift of God: Not of works, lest any man should boast" (Eph.

2:8–9). When Christ died for us, we were afforded to receive that precious gift.
- **Sword of the Spirit**—The sword of the Spirit is the Word of God that we must use to thwart against what the devil says. "For the word of God *is* quick, and powerful, and sharper than any twoedged sword, piercing even to the dividing asunder of soul and spirit, and of the joints and marrow, and *is* a discerner of the thoughts and intents of the heart" (Heb. 4:12).

Take time to pray this:

Prayer

Holy Spirit, I ask that You help me to keep each piece of Your armor on as I go throughout my day, every day. When a piece is about to fall off or is not securely in place, assist me to adjust it.

Although I may have to fight off the enemy with these pieces, I know, Jesus, that You won the ultimate fight when You died on the cross for me. For this, I thank You today and forever. Amen.

Course of Action

How do you plan to use each piece of the armor of God? Write out how you plan to implement this into your life.

Day 18: Spiritual Warfare

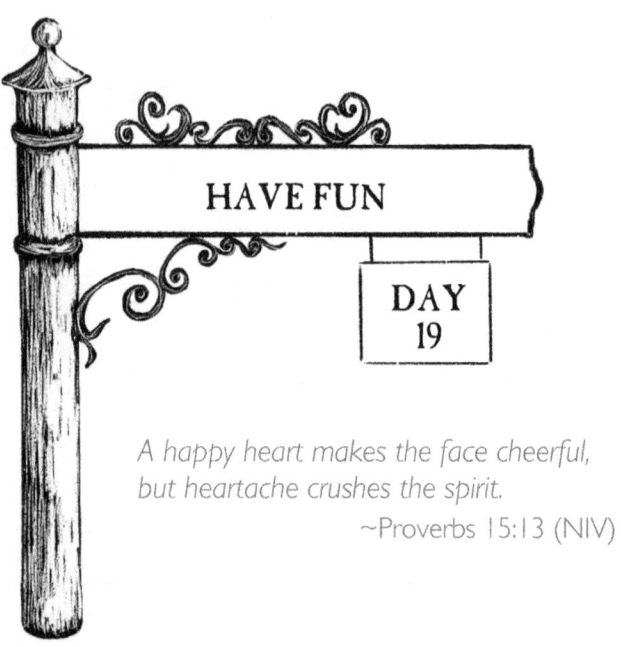

HAVE FUN

DAY 19

*A happy heart makes the face cheerful,
but heartache crushes the spirit.*

~Proverbs 15:13 (NIV)

Just imagine—you gaze out on a tropical island view of crystal-clear, green-blue waters of the ocean. You relax under a beach umbrella, and warm sun rays slightly kiss your skin. Sound good?

Most people who know me know I love to travel. Traveling to new places and learning about different cultures both fascinate me. God created so much beauty in the world; it would be a shame if I didn't embrace and enjoy it.

But I remember periods in my life where work-life balance felt almost impossible, and I wasn't enjoying my world. My work schedule left me feeling burned-out, without enough time for the

Day 19: Have Fun

people I love, or to do the things that I love. I was in an all-work and no-play scenario for a time.

God wants us to enjoy life. It's not all work and drudgery, but we can be guilty of forgetting that. I learned to consciously carve out time for fun. Life is about balance.

To enjoy life to the fullest, set aside time for good, clean fun. Fun doesn't have to be expensive as traveling out of the country. Fun can be found in simple pleasures, such as discovering a new hobby, spending time with loved ones, even going out to a new restaurant.

I will advise a few caveats. It's vital to learn to have fun within your means, because it will not be fun anymore if you go broke—read Day 21, "Financially Fit" if you need work on this area! And even with affordable, good, clean fun, problems can arise if we overemphasize fun without keeping in mind our purpose and doing our God-given assignments. If you think you might have a problem with playing too much, go back and review Day 13, and think about how the fun you have can fit in with your purpose.

Be grateful: as a single woman, you have some advantages others do not. You don't have to consult a spouse about where you should go. You can go on vacation without worrying about who is going to watch the kids. You have the blessing and gift of precious freedom and time to explore new and exciting things. Don't waste it!

Ecclesiastes 5:19 says, "Moreover, when God gives someone wealth and possessions, and the ability to enjoy them, to accept their lot and be happy in their toil—this is a gift of God" (NIV). God wants us to enjoy the resources that He provides for us. Sometimes we become so busy that we forget to have fun and enjoy the fruits of our labor. But you: don't forget! Go, have fun!

Take time to pray this:

Prayer

Dear Father, I ask that you show me ways to have good, clean fun. Grant me the resources to afford to do my heart's desires. In Jesus' name. Amen.

Course of Action

Write down some ways you would like to have fun. Remember, fun doesn't have to be expensive: it can be something as simple as reading a novel that you have been eyeing in a bookstore or library.

How will you commit to have fun today?

_____
_____
_____
_____
_____

Day 19: Have Fun

Now, write out what contentment looks like to you.

_____
_____
_____
_____
_____
_____

How will you stay on this road to contentment?

_____
_____
_____
_____
_____
_____
_____
_____
_____
_____
_____
_____

DOING KIND DEEDS

DAY 20

And be ye kind one to another, tenderhearted, forgiving one another, even as God for Christ's sake hath forgiven you.

~Ephesians 4:32 (KJV)

A few years ago, I was at the doctor's office because of a really bad cold that wouldn't go away. As I was signing in at the front desk, I couldn't help but overhear a patient's conversation with a receptionist. The patient was not able to pay her medical bill. At that moment, I felt led to pay her bill. I told the receptionist that I would pay her bill because I knew what it was like not to be able to afford it. I had the money and she needed the money, so I felt it was only right to help her out. I had never seen the woman before, but that didn't stop me from doing what I needed to do.

Day 20: Doing Kind Deeds

This isn't to brag about what I did. I share it to show how little acts of kindness can make this world a better place. In the end, the woman was so grateful that she began crying at the generosity extended towards her. I explained to her it was because I felt led by God to do it, so it's all Him.

When you get a nudge from the Holy Spirit to do something or say something kind to someone, do it! You never know what that act of kindness will mean to someone. It may lead someone to Christ. It may give a person hope when they have lost all hope.

The act of kindness can be something as simple as complimenting a person on their outfit or hairstyle. As women we sometimes act as if we are in competition with each other. We may turn up our noses at people because we start to feel insecurities. In our minds, we think they know how to dress better, or they may wear fancier hairstyles, etc. But what if we just compliment others? Just because someone's hair is done nicely or she wears cute clothes doesn't mean she thinks she is better than you. It certainly doesn't mean that she is better than you.

We can choose kindness. We can choose compassion. Jesus did.

"Teacher, this woman was caught in the act of adultery," the Pharisees and scribes told Jesus as they brought the woman to Him. "In the Law, Moses commanded us to stone such women. Now, what do you say?"

Jesus responded by writing on the ground, "Let any one of you who is without sin be the first to throw a stone at her" (John 8:7 NIV).

Each one of the Pharisees began to walk away and Jesus then spoke to the woman. He told her that He didn't condemn her and encouraged her to leave her life of sin. How easily Jesus could have agreed with the others and told them to stone her, but instead he chose to be kind and compassionate.

Isn't that how we are supposed to be today with each other? If someone comes to us and we disagree with them, we shouldn't lash out. Instead, we should respond in a gentle manner.

Being kind is not being a pushover. It doesn't mean that you allow people to take advantage of you. Sometimes we fear that if we are kind, people will think that we are weak. But no: it just means that your delivery through words or actions is not harsh. We can kindly get our point across without yelling or being rude. Kindness is being a confident, assertive, and godly woman.

Let's pray.

Prayer

Father God, I ask that You impress me to do kind deeds towards others. When I'm tempted to act with unseemly behavior, please grant me the spirit of kindness. Allow kindness to flow through my words and deeds. Your examples of kindness throughout Your Word and in my life have shown

Day 20: Doing Kind Deeds

me that I am to follow this same path. In Jesus' name. Amen.

Course of Action

First think of a time someone has extended an unexpected kindness to you. What happened, and how did that act of kindness change your day?

The next time you see a person in need, offer some type of assistance. Offer a kind compliment to someone that you may not have otherwise done. What other acts of kindness can you see yourself performing?

FINANCIALLY FIT

DAY 21

There is treasure to be desired and oil in the dwelling of the wise; but a foolish man spendeth it up.
~Proverbs 21:20 (KJV)

Megan, a shopaholic, went to Nordstrom to purchase the Michael Kors leather clutch bag she had been eyeing for months. As the cashier rang up the bag, she announced that the clutch was over seven hundred dollars. Most of Megan's credit cards were maxed out because of excessive spending, so Megan quickly decided to resort to using her last good credit card. She purchased the bag and left the store temporarily satisfied after a beautiful day of retail therapy.

Megan represents many today who spend more money than they bring in, causing them to rack up debt. While I am not against purchasing name

Day 21: Financially Fit

brands, in my opinion, it's important for us to make sure that we are not overspending. If a person has the resources, certainly they can spend more than the average person; however, even if we have that ability, we still need to be responsible.

Proverbs 21:20 says, "There is treasure to be desired and oil in the dwelling of the wise; but a foolish man spendeth it up." This passage of Scripture discusses the difference between the foolish and the wise in how they deal with their money. The wise save for rainy days and don't overspend, whereas the foolish spends all he has and doesn't save. God is our resource for everything that we have, so shouldn't we be responsible in how we handle what He gives us?

It can be enticing to buy the latest and most expensive brands, but we should ask ourselves, "Can I really afford this? Is this item filling a need or desire?" When we feel tempted to overspend, we should also ask, "Am I trying to fill a hole for a desire for a relationship with stuff?" For some single people, they may feel since they are not in a relationship that they deserve to buy this item even though they know they cannot afford it.

The key is to think about the future because life has unexpected turns where we may need extra money. As a single person, you may want to buy a house, save for that future wedding, travel, etc., and if you learn to save some of the resources that you have, you will be investing in future blessings.

Let's pray.

Prayer

Holy Spirit, teach me the difference between wants and needs. I ask that You give me godly wisdom on managing my finances. When life brings financial challenges, remind me that You will provide all of my needs (Phil. 4:19) as You are my true source. In Jesus' name. Amen.

Course of Action

If managing money is not something you are good at, find some of the many available resources on how to become financially fit (websites, classes, books). Ask a trusted friend or family member who is knowledgeable on the subject to help you.

Now, answer this question:

Am I managing my finances well?
_____ Yes _____ No

What steps do I need to take to continue my good financial management or improve my financial responsibility?

_____
_____
_____
_____
_____

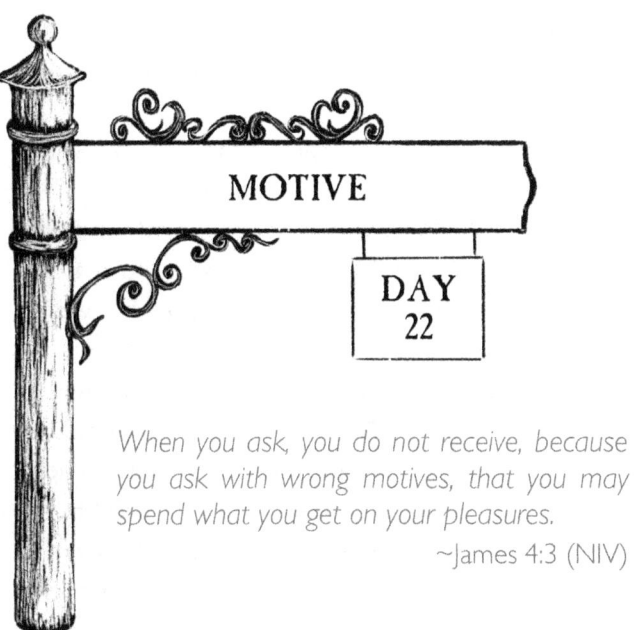

MOTIVE

DAY 22

When you ask, you do not receive, because you ask with wrong motives, that you may spend what you get on your pleasures.

~James 4:3 (NIV)

"I'm finally getting married!" exclaimed Tanya to her best friend Maria. Tanya, in her early twenties, finally met her prince charming. He was a doctor and very handsome.

"Oh my goodness! I'm so happy for you. You are finally getting to marry the man that you love." Maria smiled and hugged her friend.

Maria noticed that Tanya didn't smile at that last statement, so Maria asked her, "You do love him, right?"

"Love is so overrated, Maria. I'm finally getting out of my parents' house and I know that he is a good man and well-off financially. So, who needs love?"

"Tanya! How can you say that? Love is very important in a relationship," Maria stated, resting her hand on her friend's shoulder.

"Maria, this is my decision. I thought you would be happy for me," Tanya said angrily.

Maria didn't know what to say to her friend. She knew Tanya was making a big mistake to marry a man whom she didn't love, all for the wrong motives.

As a Christian single, there have been times I have asked myself, "Why do I want to get married?" I must admit that my motives have not always been for the right reasons. As God began to reveal to me the wrong motives for getting married, He began to restore my heart to desire a husband not for selfish reasons, but to ultimately be in God's will.

Many, like Tanya, want to get married to be financially secure. Others want to be rid of societal pressures to get married. Some simply want to have a companion—a person to share life with. For some, they want to finally have sex the right way.

In everything we want out of life, we should always check our motives. We should check our motives for not only marriage, but for every aspect of our lives whether for careers, finances, children, etc.

In James 4:3, James explained to the Jewish Christians that when they ask for something, they receive not because they were asking with wrong motives. We need the same message today. Even though something we want can be a good thing, if

Day 22: Motive

we ask with the wrong motives, it's not good and God doesn't honor that. God ordained marriage, but if all we want is to get married for selfish gain, how do we truly expect God to bless us?

Let's pray.

Prayer

Father God, I pray that my motives towards the works that I do in this life and the desires that I have in my heart are pure before You. If they are not, Holy Spirit, please reveal it to me. In Jesus' name, I pray. Amen.

Course of Action

What are some of your desires? Are they coming from pure motives? If not, then ask God to help you.

Make a list of these desires and think about why you really want to have them.

_____
_____
_____
_____
_____
_____

Dear God, What About Me?

It's okay to be honest, because guess what? God already knows your true motives. Ask God to redirect your motives to motives that are pure.

LOVE

DAY 23

A new command I give you: Love one another. As I have loved you, so you must love one another. By this everyone will know that you are my disciples, if you love one another.

~John 13:34–35 (NIV)

The greatest demonstration of God's love for us was when Jesus died on the cross. Jesus makes a very powerful statement in John 10:18, "No one takes [my life] from me, but I lay it down of my own accord. I have authority to lay it down and authority to take it up again. This command I received from my Father" (NIV). Jesus could have stopped the whole crucifixion because He is the Son of God. Instead, He stated that the Scriptures must be fulfilled and through that fulfilment, lives will be forever changed.

Let's go even deeper. Jesus, the King of Kings, came into flesh in a sin-tainted world to redeem back mankind when He didn't even have to leave

His throne in Heaven. He could have redeemed us in so many other ways, but no, He sacrificed Himself so that we might have life. Keep in mind that He did this even while we were yet sinners. A love like that is so unfathomable and indescribable that it sometimes leaves people thinking that His message of grace is too good to be true.

We can be selfish when we deal with others. If a person hurts us, we may start acting indifferently and may not want to be bothered. But with God, His love is unconditional. Even when we hurt Him by our choices, He is always there waiting for us to run back to Him.

Take time to pray this:

Prayer

Father God, I ask that You infuse me continually with your Holy Spirit and Your love that I may be able to demonstrate the love that You have displayed in my life. Allow the fruit of love to continuously be portrayed in my actions and my words, even towards my enemies. I thank You, God, for Your special love towards me because I know that there is no one who can love me the way that You do. You are my love and my heart, and for that, I am forever grateful. In Jesus' name. Amen.

Course of Action

As believers, we should strive to demonstrate the same type of love and grace that God extends to us

Day 23: Love

to the people in our lives. Some of us are at different levels when it comes to showing love to others, and it's okay. Ask God to show you how to demonstrate His love towards others in everyday life.

And let us not be weary in well doing: for in due season we shall reap, if we faint not.

~Galatians 6:9 (KJV)

DAY 24 — PATIENCE

"**I want it now!**"

Have you ever felt like this? I don't always want to wait. Sometimes, I want something that day, or, if I'm feeling particularly patient, within the same year.

When I've had to wait, God has shown me how to wait on Him and He has developed my patience. Imagine what we would be like if we never developed patience. We would be spoiled, ungrateful people, never learning how to appreciate the gifts God gives to us. By developing the fruit of patience, the Holy Spirit sharpens our character to be more like Him. God wants us to learn how to

Day 24: Patience

wait well. To do that, we must learn how to be patient.

If we don't learn to have patience, we may find ourselves making bad choices in life. We may find ourselves marrying a person God didn't intend for us to marry.

An example of what happens when we refuse to wait on God is found in the story of Abraham and Sarah. God promised Abraham that he would have a son. When it seemed like the promise was never going to come to fruition, Sarah told Abraham to sleep with their maidservant, Hagar, so that she could have children through her. Abraham agreed because he probably thought that this was how God was going to bless him with his offspring. Hagar had a son, Ishmael, but he was not the promised seed that God intended.

God eventually gave Sarah and Abraham a son, Isaac, but as result of not being patient, there was conflict between the two families.

Remember: God works in the impossible. Even though a prayer request or desire that God promised you may seem to take a long time, God will fulfill it.

Let's pray.

Prayer

Father God, I ask that patience continue to grow in my life. When I become weary in waiting for Your promises, continuously restore me. In Your Word,

Dear God, What About Me?

You promise that "in due season we shall reap, if we faint not." "For all the promises of God in him are yea, and in him Amen, unto the glory of God by us" (2 Cor. 1:20 KJV). In Jesus' name. Amen

Course of Action

What are you having problems with being patient with in your life? Write down these things and ask God to help you with them.

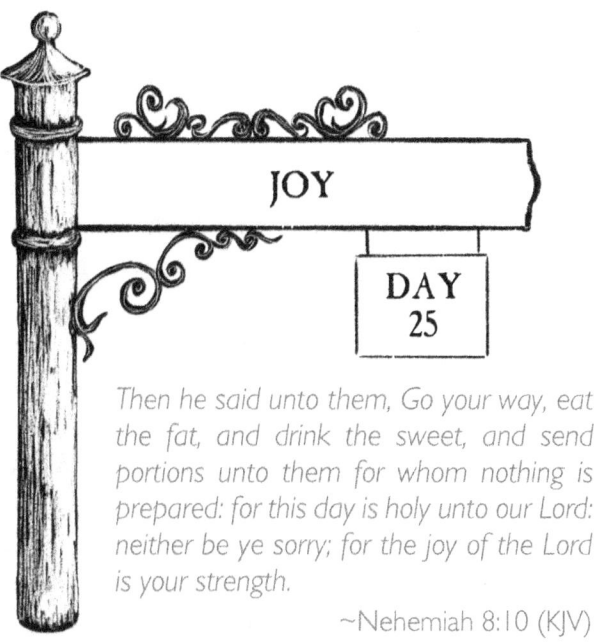

JOY

DAY 25

Then he said unto them, Go your way, eat the fat, and drink the sweet, and send portions unto them for whom nothing is prepared: for this day is holy unto our Lord: neither be ye sorry; for the joy of the Lord is your strength.

~Nehemiah 8:10 (KJV)

Her husband died from cancer, and she sits looking at his body. From what I can see, she doesn't shed a tear outwardly, but I know deep down she is hurting that this man she knew for most of her life is no longer here. As she walks down the aisle on the day of the funeral, she carries herself with grace and poise. Someone asks her how is she going through all of this, and her reply is simply, "The joy of the Lord is my strength."

Her statement will always remain with me. It is easy to have joy when life is going well, but how is it possible to have joy when tragic circumstances stare you in the face? As a young person, I've wondered this, but then God spoke to me and gave me this revelation.

When it seems like you are all alone, and when it seems like everything is taken from you, then God is trying to say, "If you have Me, I am enough." In this place, you will finally unlock the truth to the statement, "The joy of the Lord is my strength."

He is trying to get you to the place to stop depending on people and things for the source of your joy. When you felt as if life was going great, you thought that material assets and people were your joy. In the face of tragedy, He strips that away so that the fruit of your joy can grow.

In other words, true joy is never dependent on circumstances, but on God alone. By spending time with Him and allowing Him to fill your heart, He will produce joy. Your joy rests also in the fact that the world we live in is temporary and awaiting us is eternity with our Heavenly Father.

Let's pray.

Prayer

Dear Heavenly Father, I ask that You replenish me with Your joy on a daily basis when the enemy tries to rob me of Your joy. Remind me that joy doesn't come from material possessions or even from people but only from You. You are the source of my joy now and forever more. In Jesus' name, I pray. Amen.

Day 25: Joy

Course of Action

Do you have joy in your life?

Confess the Scripture Nehemiah 8:10 (found at the beginning of the devotional for today) daily if you struggle with having joy.

> *The joy of the Lord
> is my strength.*

FAITH

DAY 26

Now faith is the substance of things hoped for, the evidence of things not seen.
~Hebrews 11:1 (KJV)

When we become believers in Christ, it is *through faith* that we are saved. Most of us know this, but what about when we are believing in God for everyday desires to find a spouse, have children, buy a house, etc.? What about when fulfilment of those desires seems to be taking a long time? It is important to hold onto faith in our relationship with God even when life doesn't make sense. We sometimes struggle with this because we either feel like we must not deserve that thing we want or that God won't do what He says. We need to have the type of faith that believes that all things are possible through Christ Jesus.

Day 26: Faith

Faith unlocks the doors of the impossible. How do we gain such faith when situations seem impossible?

Here are some ways to do this.

First, know that Jesus loves you and wants the best for you. No matter what the outcome, God is in control. Sometimes we have faith to have things that are not good for us, and in those circumstances, God may not give those desires to us. Other times, He may allow them. Once I wanted to go on a study abroad trip, and I didn't have the funds to go. I prayed to the Lord believing that He could make the situation possible, if it was His will. In the end, I was able to afford to go on the trip. He gave me the wisdom on how to raise the money. I believed in my heart that even if He didn't allow me to go, I knew He was still capable.

Second, ask God to help you. Read stories of people in the Bible who struggled through rough seasons. Joseph, for example, was sold into slavery by his brothers. Later, he was sent to prison after Potiphar's wife accused him of trying to have sex with her (Gen. 37 and 39). Naomi lost her husband and two sons (Ruth 1–4). She was so distraught that she no longer wanted to be called *Naomi* but instead *Mara* which means "the Almighty has made my life very bitter" (Ruth 1:20 NIV). Joseph and Naomi had to have faith to go through their rough seasons to get the blessings of God. Listen to testimonies of others. When you do this, you start to understand that if God can do it for this person, He can do it for you as well.

Let's pray.

Prayer

Father God, I ask that You help to continue to grow my faith that I will be pleasing to You. Don't allow unbelief to reign in my heart. You are the author and finisher of my faith, so I allow You to grow this fruit within me. In Jesus' name. Amen.

Course of Action

Write how you plan to increase your faith.

_____
_____
_____
_____
_____

What are ways you plan to increase your faith when it comes to wanting a spouse? Write below.

_____
_____
_____
_____
_____

SELF-CONTROL

DAY 27

> ...[D]enying ungodliness and worldly lusts, we should live soberly, righteously, and godly, in this present world.
> ~Titus 2:12 (KJV)

The soft, golden brown, white chocolate Macadamia cookies attractively boxed and placed on shelf in a popular grocery store beckoned me to buy them. I stood there as my mind kept playing ping-pong with the thoughts of my waistline on one side and the taste and gratification of the cookies as the opponent. Sweets have always been my biggest weakness and the road to self-control in this area of my life has been quite bumpy, sometimes with wins of saying *no* and other losses of saying *yes*.

Most of us know the story of Cain and Abel. The two brothers brought their offerings before God. God respected Abel's offering but didn't favor

Cain's offerings. As a result, Cain became angry with and jealous of Abel. Cain didn't control his anger and jealousy, and he ended up killing his brother. Now, if Cain would have asked God to help with his anger and had he been humble, I'm sure the circumstances would have ended differently.

Self-control is listed as a fruit of the Spirit in Galatians 5:22–23. In the King James Version, it is listed as *temperance*. Merriam-Webster's dictionary defines self-control as "restraint exercised over one's own impulses, emotions, or desires." Self-control is vital in the life of a believer because the world flaunts all types of enticing things that may be harmful. If you truly desire to live according to the Word of God, God will enable you to have self-control: we can't do this completely on our own.

Imagine if no one exercised self-control in any area of their lives. When somebody makes us mad, we may punch them in the nose and with that comes consequences such as having someone putting out a restraining order against you. Or what about the government? We probably wouldn't have a government or any type of order and control. In other words, our lives would be in total chaos because we would be acting only with our emotions and feelings.

Let's pray.

Day 27: Self-Control

Prayer

Father God, I ask that You help me to be self-controlled in _____ *(state area(s) you need help in)*. I admit that it isn't easy to control this area of my life, but with Your help, I know all things are possible.

When my flesh wants to rise up, speak to my heart on how to overcome the situation. In Jesus' name. Amen.

Course of Action

Do you struggle with self-control in certain areas of your life? List your areas of struggle and ask God to help you.

PRAISE AND WORSHIP

DAY 28

Ascribe to the LORD the glory due his name; worship the LORD in the splendor of holiness.

~Psalm 29:2 (NIV)

The worship team prepares for Sunday worship. The music plays and the worship leader's strong tenor voice sings, "Walking around these walls / I thought by now they'd fall / But You have never failed me yet. / Waiting for change to come…".[1] As the other worship team members sing, the atmosphere slowly transforms into one of worship.

My eyes scan around. I see a look of total concentration on people's faces, some with their eyes closed, hands raised high, not worrying about

---

[1] Steven Furtick, Matt Redmon, Mack Brock & Chris Brown. *Do It Again.* There is a Cloud. (Charlotte, NC: Elevation Church, 2017), https://genius.com/Elevation-worship-do-it-again-lyrics.

Day 28: Praise and Worship

who is watching them. The atmosphere is one of complete freedom.

My own eyes shut as I concentrate on the words of the song. My heart begins to pour out gratitude to my Heavenly Father for His amazing love. My arms raise, and in that moment, it's just me and Jesus. I'm filled with such exhilaration that I feel as if I'm floating. My mind is not flooded with circumstances and problems. I am simply in awe of my Heavenly Father.

There's something about praising and worshiping God for who He is without worrying about what is going on around us. So, unsatisfied single: worship God even when you may be surrounded by life's trials! When you worship in spirit and in truth, He will show up and you will be comforted. During worship, you are in communion with God. For many, God will minister to you by giving words of comfort and instruction. Allow Him to bear the worries of life, and instead concentrate solely on Him. Worship Him for who He is and not necessarily what He can do for you. Jesus, our Savior, deserves all the praise!

After a Sunday service, practice worshipping God every day. Worship is so much more than just hands raised in the air during a scheduled service. We worship Him by obeying His Word and by making Him first in our lives. Finally, we worship Him by how we treat other people.

Let's pray.

Prayer

Father God, I thank you for all that You have done for me. I thank You for dying on a rugged cross for a sinner like me. You are my King. When I'm in Your presence, speak to me as my hands are raised high and my voice shouts words of adoration. I will praise and worship You, my King and my Lord. Amen.

Course of Action

We know that we can sing songs of praise to God in church, but we can do it also in our homes, cars: anywhere. What are some of your favorite worship songs? If you don't normally sing songs of praise during your prayer time, I encourage you to sing them during this time.

What will you sing?

PEACE OF MIND

DAY 29

You will keep in perfect peace those whose minds are steadfast, because they trust in you.

~Isaiah 26:3 (NIV)

In our hectic world, there is so much bad news on the television and in newspapers. News of hurricanes, tornadoes, wildfires, devastation, poverty, and loss can rob anyone of peace. Everyday life struggles, such as stress about work, finances, children, or being single, can block the flow of peace. The Serenity prayer reminds us to not worry about things we cannot change but to alter things that we can.

*God grant me the serenity
to accept the things I cannot change;
courage to change the things I can;
and wisdom to know the difference.*

I believe that there are circumstances we allow that cause our peace to be taken away. In another category, there are situations that happen to us beyond our control. Let's consider a single woman in a relationship with a man who is physically abusive. This woman will suffer from an absence of peace. Yes, she can pray about the situation, but sometimes the answer is right there: Leave. Of course, leaving a relationship is easier said than done, but if she wants peace, she will need to change her circumstance.

Now let's consider a woman who found out that she lost her house because of a hurricane in her area. This woman had no control over this catastrophic event and doesn't have peace. If we want peace in our lives, we have to determine which category our situation is in. If we can change something in our lives to cause peace, then we should. Both women need to ask God for peace in their situations; however, one has the opportunity to change her circumstance—the woman with the boyfriend.

Take time to pray this:

Prayer

Father God, I ask that You consume me with Your peace. You said in Your Word that "The LORD gives strength to his people; the LORD blesses his people with peace" (Psalm 29:11).

Day 29: Peace of Mind

I know it's Your desire that we all have peace in our lives, so remove anything in my life that will steal the peace that You want to freely give me.

Course of Action

What are some things in your life that are robbing you of your peace? If you have the opportunity to change it, then do so. If you can't change your circumstance, then ask God to give you peace to accept it.

Write out your prayer.

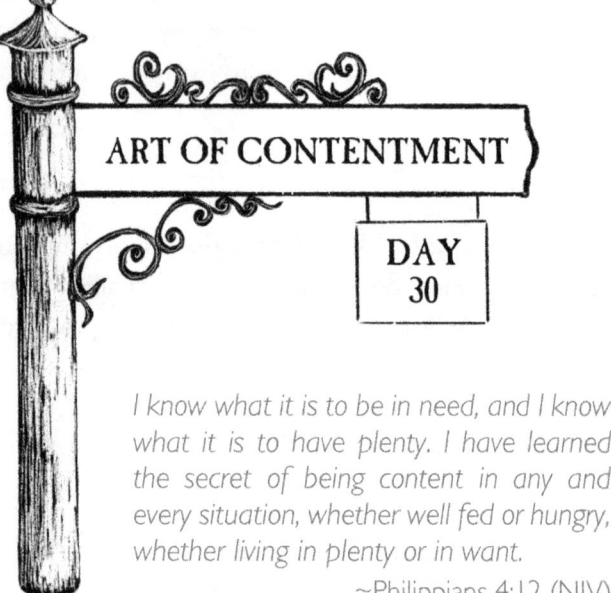

ART OF CONTENTMENT

DAY 30

I know what it is to be in need, and I know what it is to have plenty. I have learned the secret of being content in any and every situation, whether well fed or hungry, whether living in plenty or in want.

~Philippians 4:12 (NIV)

The apostle Paul was imprisoned when he wrote the words in the opening quotation to the church of Philippi. How can a person be content when in prison, when hungry, or when he is in want as Paul described? Or, let's go even deeper—let's have it hit us where we're concerned—how can a woman who wants to be married be content when single? Now, I don't know about you, but this passage of Scripture appears intimidating and seems impossible to live by. However, it can be done. Paul learned that his contentment was not in external circumstances. His contentment was in Christ.

Day 30: Art of Contentment

I've travailed on some rough roads in my life and there were times when the thought of contentment was out of the question. I wasn't where I wanted to be, and I complained. But I've learned that complaining doesn't improve things and only makes my heart more frustrated.

I have allowed God to do a new work in me. I have learned to go through times of dissatisfaction with less murmuring and complaining. His Spirit has reworked my heart. I want to be content in Christ even when it seems like everything is falling apart around me. I find the more I stay in the presence of God, the more God changes my heart to be content.

You may think: you don't know my situation. No one could be content with what I face.

Now of course, we all want things to get better when we're in a bad place. Of course no one wants negative circumstances, but I've come to the point where if I believe God has allowed a situation to happen, I am not going to fight Him on it. My mind is set that I will walk through the valley of the shadow of death because God is with me and He will provide the way out.

This is where we all have to one day come to a decision. I pray that you follow Paul's example of being content.

Let's pray.

Prayer

Lord, I ask that You that You assist me with being content with where I am in my life right now. Continuously show me that You alone are enough for me even if all of my desires are not met when I want them to be. I ask that You teach me to have a grateful heart in all situations that I may face. In Jesus' name. Amen.

Course of Action

So, how can you cultivate an attitude of contentment?

1. Be thankful for what you have in your life.

2. Stop comparing your life to others.

3. Know your purpose and fulfill it.

4. Continuously grow in Christ.

Look back over the month of devotions you've completed. How has God brought you closer to contentment in your life as a single woman?

Day 30: Art of Contentment

Conclusion

Reader,

I hope that through having read this devotional, through prayer, and through putting your faith in action, your mindset about being single has become one that reflects contentment. It's okay to want more out of life, but keep in mind that contentment is about peace of mind. While it's normal to ask, "Dear God, what about me? What about granting my desires?", God has you where He does for a reason. You can trust Him.

Before we end, I want to remind you that the journey to contentment includes the realization that our worth does not come from our relationship or marital status. Certainly, we'll never be lastingly happy in a relationship with another person until we can first be content in our relationship with God. Remember, marriage is not a destination. It is not a sign that you have made it. It is just a part of the journey called life.

If there are topics from this devotional that you continue to struggle with, I encourage you to go back over those devotions regularly. I'm the author of this book and there are definitely some things in here that I struggle with from time to time as well. But by meditating on relevant Scriptures and on God's message to me, I find I can stay on the road of contentment and peace in Him and His call and purpose in my life. I am confident that you can, too!

Let's end with a quick prayer:

> *Father God, I ask that You bless the reader of this devotional to be everything that You have called her to be. I pray that this woman will wait on You for her husband if marriage is part of Your will for her life. Allow her not to settle on just anyone to be her mate, but to be joined to someone whom she is spiritually compatible with. I believe that You called her to be a virtuous, God-pleasing woman who is created for a special purpose. Let her know that she is a jewel in Your eyes when life may tell her differently. Most importantly, I ask You to strengthen her during this season of her life. In Jesus' name, I pray. Amen.*

God bless you, woman of God, on your journey!

www.ingramcontent.com/pod-product-compliance
Lightning Source LLC
LaVergne TN
LVHW041227080426
835508LV00011B/1103